EXPANDED EDITION

Grade 2

The *How Big Is a Foot?* lesson is part of the
Picture-Perfect STEM program K–2 written by the
program authors and includes lessons from their
award-winning series.

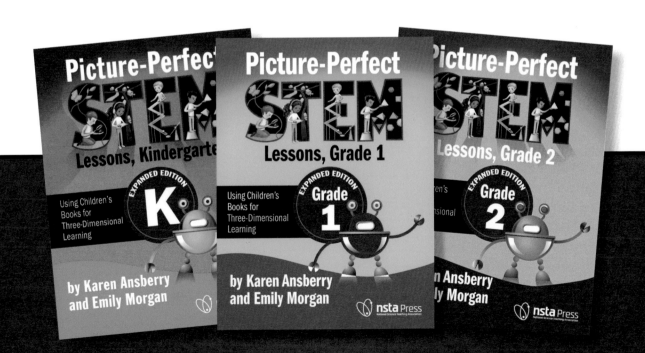

How Big Is a Foot?

Description

Learners explore the history of measurement from the ancient Egyptian use of nonstandard units to the modern-day metric system. They learn why standard measuring tools are useful and that their development was a problem-solving process that took centuries.

Alignment with the *Next Generation Science Standards*

Performance Expectation		
K-2-ETS1-1: Ask questions, make observations, and gather information about a situation that people want to change to define a simple problem that can be solved through the development of a new or improved object or tool		
Science and Engineering Practices	**Disciplinary Core Ideas**	**Crosscutting Concept**
Analyzing and Interpreting Data Analyze data from tests of an object or tool to determine if it works as intended. **Using Mathematics and Computational Thinking** Use quantitative data to compare two alternative solutions to a problem.	**ETS1.A: Defining and Delimiting Engineering Problems** A situation that people want to change or create can be approached as a problem to be solved through engineering. Such problems may have many acceptable solutions. Asking questions, making observations, and gathering information are helpful in thinking about problems. Before beginning to design a solution, it is important to clearly understand the problem.	**Scale, Proportion, and Quantity** Standard units are used to measure length.

Note: The activities in this lesson will help students move toward the performance expectations listed, which is the goal after multiple activities. However, the activities will not by themselves be sufficient to reach the performance expectations.

Contemporary research on how students learn science, reflected in the *Next Generation Science Standards* and other state standards based in *A Framework for K–12 Science Education,* requires that engineering lessons taught as part of the science curriculum provide students with opportunities to "acquire and use elements of disciplinary core ideas from physical, life, or Earth and space sciences together with elements of disciplinary core ideas from engineering design to solve design problems." (NGSS Lesson Screener, *www.nextgenscience.org/screener*)

Featured Picture Books

TITLE: *How Big Is a Foot?*
AUTHOR: **Rolf Myller**
ILLUSTRATOR: **Rolf Myller**
PUBLISHER: **Young Yearling**
YEAR: **1991**
GENRE: **Story**
SUMMARY: *The King has a problem. He wants to give the Queen a bed for her birthday, but no one knows the answer to the question "How big is a bed?"*

TITLE: *How Tall, How Short, How Faraway?*
AUTHOR: **David A. Adler**
ILLUSTRATOR: **Nancy Tobin**
PUBLISHER: **Holiday House**
YEAR: **1999**
GENRE: **Non-Narrative Information**
SUMMARY: *Colorful cartoons and easy-to-follow text introduce the history of measurement, from the ancient Egyptian system to the metric system.*

Time Needed

This lesson will take several class periods. Suggested scheduling is as follows:

Session 1: **Engage** with *How Big Is a Foot?* Read-Aloud and **Explore** with Measuring with Feet

Session 2: **Explain** with A Letter to the King

Session 3: **Explain** with *How Tall, How Short, How Faraway?* Read-Aloud and Measurement Activities

Session 4: **Elaborate** with Measuring the Playground

Session 5: **Evaluate** with A Better Way to Measure

Materials

For Measuring with Feet

• About 2 m of string or yarn (per pair of students)
• Roll of masking tape
• Yardstick

For Measurement Activities

• Meterstick
• Metric ruler (1 per student)

For Measuring the Playground

- Measuring wheel (1 per class)
- Metric ruler (per group of 4)
- Meterstick (per group of 4)
- Metric tape measure – soft, not metal (per group of 4)
- Clipboard (per group of 4)

Student Pages

- A Letter to the King
- Measuring the Playground
- A Better Way to Measure to Map a Buried Treasure
- STEM Everywhere

Background for Teachers

In this lesson, students learn how the development of standard measurements was a fascinating but lengthy problem-solving process.

Weights and measures were among the first tools invented by humans. Ancient people used their body parts and items in their surroundings as their first measuring tools. Early Egyptian and Babylonian records indicate that length was first measured with the forearm, hand, and fingers. As societies evolved, measurements became more complex. It became more and more important to be able to measure accurately time after time and to be able to reproduce the measurements in different places. By the 18th century, England had achieved a greater degree of standardization in measurement than other European countries. The English, or *customary system* of measurement, commonly used in the United States, is nearly the same as that brought by the colonists from England.

The need for a single, worldwide measurement system was recognized more than 300 years ago when a French priest named Gabriel Mouton proposed a comprehensive decimal measurement system. A century passed, however, and no action was taken. During the French Revolution, the National Assembly of France requested that the French Academy of Sciences "deduce an invariable standard for all the measures and all the weights." A system was proposed that was both simple and scientific: the *metric system*. The simplicity of the metric system is due to its being based on units of 10. The standardized structure and decimal features of the metric system made it well suited for scientific and engineering work, so it is not surprising that wide acceptance of the metric system coincided with an age of rapid technological development. By an Act of Congress in 1866, it became "lawful throughout the United States of America to employ the weights and measures of the metric system to all contracts, dealings, and court proceedings." By 1900, a total of 35 nations had accepted the metric system. Eventually, the name *Systeme Internationale d'Unites* (International System of Units) with the international abbreviation SI was given to the metric system. Although the customary system of measurement is commonly used in everyday situations in the United States, U.S. scientists primarily use the metric system (SI) in their daily work.

Adapted from: A Brief History of Measurement Systems
    www.dickeyphysics.com/Physics_Readings/History%20of%20Measurement%20Systems.pdf

In this lesson, students approach the topic of the development of standard measures as an engineering design process. They make sense of why we use standard units of measurement through reading a story that poses the problem with nonstandard units of measurement and by collecting and analyzing data from nonstandard measurements. They are engaged in the science and engineering practices (SEPs) of analyzing and interpreting data and using mathematics and computational thinking through these activities. The crosscutting concept (CCC) of scale, proportion, and quantity permeates the lesson as students compare standard and nonstandard units. The SEP of obtaining, evaluating, and communicating information comes into play as students read a nonfiction book about the history of measurement and as they communicate explanations and solutions in writing.

Learning Progressions

Below are the disciplinary core idea (DCI) grade band endpoints for grades K–2 and 3–5. These are provided to show how student understanding of the DCIs in this lesson will progress in future grade levels.

DCIs	Grades K–2	Grades 3–5
ETS1.A: Defining and Delimiting Engineering Problems	• A situation that people want to change or create can be approached as a problem to be solved through engineering. • Asking questions, making observations, and gathering information are helpful in thinking about problems. • Before beginning to design a solution, it is important to clearly understand the problem.	• Possible solutions to a problem are limited by available materials and resources (constraints). The success of a designed solution is determined by considering the desired features of a solution (criteria). Different proposals for solutions can be compared on the basis of how well each one meets the specified criteria for success or how well each takes the constraints into account.

Source: Willard, T., ed. 2015. *The NSTA quick-reference guide to the* NGSS: *Elementary school.* Arlington, VA: NSTA Press.

 engage

How Big Is a Foot? Read-Aloud

Connecting to the Common Core
Reading: Literature
KEY IDEAS AND DETAILS: 2.3

 *Inferring*

Show students the cover of the book *How Big Is a Foot? Ask*

? What can you infer from the title and illustration on the cover of this book?

Begin reading the book aloud but stop after reading, "Why was the bed too small for the Queen?" *Ask*

? Do you think it is fair that the King put the apprentice in jail? Why or why not?

National Science Teaching Association

Have students share their ideas with a partner, and then call on students to share with the class. *Ask*

? How big IS a foot?

Students will likely conclude that it depends on what you mean by "foot." Students might know that a foot is a unit of measure that is 12 inches long. But if you are talking about a person's foot, we'll have to find out!

explore

Measuring with Feet

Remind students that "the King took off his shoes and with his big feet walked carefully around the Queen. He counted that the bed must be three feet wide." Tell students that they are going to determine the length of three feet by using their own feet. Give each pair of students about 2 m of yarn or string. Then demonstrate the steps for measuring three "feet":

1. Have your partner hold the end of the string where the back of your heel touches the floor.

2. Place one foot right in front of the other for three steps, and then freeze.

3. Have your partner stretch the string to the big toe of your third step.

4. Cut the string. It will now represent the length of your three "feet."

5. Attach a piece of masking tape with your name on it to one end of the string.

6. Hang your string from the board.

7. Help your partner measure his or her three "feet."

When all students have hung their strings on the board, compare the various lengths. *Ask*

? Are all of the strings the same length? Why or why not?

MEASURING THREE "FEET"

> **SEP: Analyzing and Interpreting Data**
> Analyze data from tests of an object or tool to determine if it works as intended.

Hold up a yardstick and *ask*

? How many feet are in a yard? (Students may know there are three feet in a yard.)

? How does your string compare to three feet as measured by a yardstick?

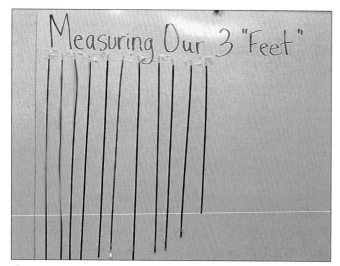

COMPARING THE STRINGS

explain

A Letter to the King

Connecting to the Common Core
Writing
TEXT TYPES AND PURPOSES: 2.1

 *Writing*

Refer back to the book *How Big Is a Foot?* and revisit the question:

? Do you think it is fair that the King put the apprentice in jail? Why or why not?

? What advice would you give the King about how he might be able to get a bed the right size for the Queen?

On the A Letter to the King student page, have students write a persuasive letter to the King about why he should let the apprentice out of jail. Ask them to explain why the bed is too small for the Queen and what he could do to get a bed that is the right size. Have students share their letters with a partner. Read the student letters to assess whether students understand that the bed is too

short because of the difference in foot size between the King and the apprentice. Students should also provide reasonable advice for getting a bed the right size.

Next, read the rest of the book to students. *Ask*

? How does the apprentice's solution in the book compare to the advice you gave in your letter?

? What measuring tool was created to solve the problem? (a model of the King's foot sculpted out of marble)

? Is there more than one correct solution? (yes)

? What are some other ways that the King could have had the bed built the right size? (by using a standard measurement tool with more precise markings)

? What tool would you use today to measure a bed? (tape measure, meterstick, ruler)

explain

How Tall, How Short, How Faraway? Read-Aloud

Connecting to the Common Core
Reading: Informational Text
INTEGRATION OF KNOWLEDGE AND IDEASS: 2.9

🦇 *Making Connections: Text to Text*

Show students the cover of *How Tall, How Short, How Faraway?* Ask

? What do you think this book is about?

Hold up *How Tall, How Short, How Faraway?* and *How Big Is a Foot?* Ask

? What do you think these two books might have in common? (Examples of answers include that both are about measurement and about people's height.)

National Science Teaching Association

Ask students to signal when they hear or see any connections between the two books. Then read aloud pages 1–19 of *How Tall, How Short, How Faraway?* (ending after "5,280 feet are 1 mile"), stopping to discuss any text-to-text connections. Students may point out some of the following connections:

How Tall, How Short, How Faraway?	*How Big Is a Foot?*
Ancient Egyptians measured with their hands and arms (digits, cubits, palms, spans).	The King measured with his feet.
Measuring with hands and arms caused problems with getting accurate measurements.	Measuring with different-sized feet caused problems in getting a bed the right size for the Queen.
In the past, people often used their leader's or king's cubit or steps as a standard.	The apprentice decided to use the King's foot as a standard to remake the bed.
People made measuring sticks the size of their king's cubit or steps.	The apprentice made an exact marble copy of the King's foot and measured with it.

Measurement Activities

Connecting to the Common Core
Mathematics
2.MD.A.2

> **SEP: Using Mathematics and Computational Thinking**
> Use quantitative data to compare two alternative solutions to a problem.

Challenge students by *asking*

? Can you measure the length of my desk without a ruler?

As a class, brainstorm a list of ways that you could measure the desk without using any traditional measuring tools. Then *ask*

? How did the ancient Egyptians measure out a span? (A span is the distance from the tip of your thumb to the end of your little finger with your hand stretched wide.)

Make the following data table on the board:

Length of Desk		
Names	Spans	

MEASURING THE DESK IN SPANS

? Why did we get different answers for the length of the desk in spans? (Each person's span is a different size.)

? Why do you think the span is no longer used for measuring length? (It is not an accurate measurement because the length of the span varies from person to person.)

Connecting to the Common Core
Reading: Informational Text
KEY IDEAS AND DETAILS: 2.1

Go back to *How Tall, How Short, How Faraway?* and read from page 20 ("The metric system was first proposed over 300 years ago …") to page 31 ("People have been measuring things for thousands of years."). After reading, state that in different times and parts of the world, there have been many systems of measurement. *Ask*

? What are the two systems of measurement most widely used today? (the customary, also known as the English system, and the metric system)

SEP: Analyzing and Interpreting Data
Analyze data from tests of an object or tool to determine if it works as intended.

Call on a student to measure your desk with his or her hand span. Write that student's name and his or her number of spans on the data table. Call on another student who is noticeably taller or shorter than the first student to measure the desk in his or her spans. Write that number of spans on the data table. Then measure the desk using your own hand span, and write that number of spans on the data table. *Ask*

? Which is the correct answer for the length of my desk? (Students should begin to understand that there is no "correct" answer in spans.)

FINDING SOMETHING ONE METER LONG

National Science Teaching Association

Explain that the units used in these systems are called standard units. *Standard units* are units of measurement that are accepted and used by most people. Some examples of standard units are feet, inches, pounds, centimeters, meters, grams, and liters. The other type of units is *nonstandard units*, which are everyday objects that can be used to obtain a measurement. Examples include spans, cubits, paces, and digits.

Explain that most people around the world, as well as scientists everywhere, use the metric system because it is simpler and less confusing than the customary system. Explain that, although the metric system was invented over 200 years ago, the United States has not entirely switched over to it. Some metric units are grams, kilograms, liters, centimeters, and meters. *Ask*

? What things do you know of that are measured in metric units? (Examples include 2 l bottles of soda, 100 m dash, grams of fat in food, distances in kilometers, and kilometers per hour on a speedometer.)

Connecting to the Common Core
Mathematics
2.MD.A.1

Give each pair of students a meterstick and a metric ruler. Have students use these tools to find something in the room that is about a centimeter long and something that is about a meter long. Next, label the third column on the data table "centimeters" and call on a student to measure your desk in centimeters with a meterstick. Write that student's name and the measurement on the data table. Call on another student to measure the desk with the meterstick. Write that measurement on the

COMPARING SPANS AND CENTIMETERS

data table. Then measure the desk yourself with a meterstick and write that measurement on the data table. *Ask*

? Why were the answers so different for the length of the desk in spans yet all the same for the length of the desk in centimeters? (Each person's span is a different size, but a centimeter is always the same size.

elaborate

Measuring the Playground

Connecting to the Common Core
Mathematics
2.MD.A.1

Tell students that an important part of using standard measurements is having the proper tools and using them correctly. *Ask*

? What are some of the tools we have used so far to make standard measurements? (rulers and metersticks)

? Would a ruler or meterstick be a good tool for measuring the circumference of (or distance around) the trunk of a tree or someone's head? (No, because they are flat and can't bend.)

Show students a metric tape measure and demonstrate how it can be used to measure things that are not flat because the tape is flexible. Model how to measure the circumference of something in the classroom that is round – like a student's head – or go outdoors and measure the circumference of a tree. *Ask*

? Would a tape measure be a good tool for measuring the distance from our classroom to the playground? (It is likely not long enough. Students might suggest marking the length of the tape measure at different points and measuring from there over and over again, but with that method, it is difficult to be exact.)

Next, show students a measuring wheel and model how it is used to measure long distances. Explain that all these tools are used to measure length. They were designed by engineers to be easy to use, precise, and suitable for different situations. There are many other types of measuring tools to measure things like weight, volume, temperature, time, and so on, but this lesson just focuses on length. Explain that one of the most important things you can do to make sure you are taking precise measurements is to begin measuring at zero on the tool. Some rulers, metersticks, and tape measures begin with zero at the tip and others have some space before zero. Model where to find zero on all the measuring tools you are using for this activity. For the measuring wheel, model how to check that the device starts at zero before measuring.

> **SEP: Analyzing and Interpreting Data**
> Analyze data from tests of an object or tool to determine if it works as intended.

Give each group of four students a metric ruler, meterstick, metric tape measure, the Measuring the Playground student page, and a clipboard. Tell them that they are going to go to the playground (or the gym) to measure things using these tools. On the way to the playground, use the measuring wheel to measure the distance to the playground from your room or from the exit. Groups can take turns using the measuring wheel.

Optional: For fun, you may even want to try some high-tech measurement apps such as the Tape Measure App, Measure by Google, Measure by Apple, Ruler App, or Smart Measure.

After students practice measuring, have groups share some of the measurements they took and how they decided which tool to use to take those length measurements.

MEASURING ON THE PLAYGROUND

10

evaluate

A Better Way to Measure

Connecting to the Common Core
Writing
TEXT TYPES AND PURPOSES: 2.1

Writing

Review what students have learned about the history of measurement and the need for standard measuring tools. Then distribute the assessment student page, A Better Way to Measure. Correct responses may include the following:

1. The pirates disagree because, when they measured the distance to the treasure, they each used their own paces. One is tall and one is short, so their paces are different lengths.

2. The pirates could measure in feet, yards, or meters.

3. We wouldn't know the exact distance to anything or anyplace.

> **SEP: Using Mathematics and Computational Thinking**
> Use quantitative data to compare two alternative solutions to a problem.

STEM Everywhere

Give students the STEM Everywhere student page as a way to involve their families and extend their learning. They can do the activity with an adult helper and share their results with the class. If students do not have access to internet at home, you may choose to have them complete this activity at school.

Opportunities for Differentiated Instruction

This box lists questions and challenges related to the lesson that students may select to research, investigate, or innovate. Students may also use the questions as examples to help them generate their own questions. These questions can help you move your students from the teacher-directed investigation to engaging in the science and engineering practices in a more student-directed format.

Extra Support

For students who are struggling to meet the lesson objectives, provide a question and guide them in the process of collecting research or help them design procedures or solutions.

Extensions

For students with high interest or who have already met the lesson objectives, have them choose a question (or pose their own question), conduct their own research, and design their own procedures or solutions.

Continued

After selecting one of the questions in the box or formulating their own question, students can individually or collaboratively make predictions, design investigations or surveys to test their predictions, collect evidence, devise explanations, design solutions, or examine related resources. They can communicate their findings through a science notebook, at a poster session or gallery walk, or by producing a media project.

Research

Have students brainstorm researchable questions:

? Which countries have not adopted the metric system as their official system of measurement? Why?

? How long is a marathon and what is the story behind it?

? What are some of the abbreviations for length measurements (centimeters, kilometers, inches, feet, miles)?

Investigate

Have students brainstorm testable questions to be solved through science or math:

? How tall is everyone in your family? Order them from shortest to tallest.

? Connect 10 small paper clips and use them to measure things around your room. Do paper clips make a good measuring tool? Why or why not?

? Design a way to compare the size of your "pace" (every two steps) to the "pace" of your friends. How do they compare?

Innovate

Have students brainstorm problems to be solved through engineering:

? What objects (that are always the same size) could be used to create a new way to measure? How would you use them?

? Can you create a scale model of your room?

? Can you make a scale drawing of the playground?

Website

 Ozomatli: "Measure It!" from PBS Kids Rock
www.pbslearningmedia.org/
resource/4c3ca5c0-0e33-4504-8a16-
f6c29c9730f7/ozomatli-measure-it-pbs-
kids-rocks-video

More Books to Read

Cleary, B. P. 2009. *How long or how wide? A measuring guide.* Minneapolis: Millbrook Press.
Summary: Part of the Math is CATegorical series, this book is a fun introduction to all the ways we measure length.

Jenkins, S. 2011. *Actual size.* New York: Houghton Mifflin.
Summary: With his colorful collage illustrations, Jenkins shows the actual sizes of many interesting animals. Some pages show the entire animal, whereas others show only a part of the animal.

Leedy, L. 2000. *Measuring penny.* New York: Square Fish.
Summary: Lisa learns about the mathematics of measuring by measuring her dog Penny with all sorts of units, including pounds, inches, dog biscuits, and cotton swabs.

Nagda, A. W. and Bickel, C. 2000. *Tiger math: Learning to graph from a baby tiger.* New York: Henry Holt.
Summary: At the Denver Zoo, a Siberian tiger cub named T. J. is orphaned when he is only a few weeks old. The zoo staff raises him, feeding him by hand until he is able to eat on his own and return to the tiger exhibit. The story is accompanied by graphs that chart T. J.'s growth, showing a wonderful example of real-world mathematics.

Pluckrose, H. 2018. *Length.* Chicago: Children's Press.
Summary: Photographs and simple text introduce the concept of length and ways to measure it.

Sweeny, J. 2019. *Me and the measure of things.* Decorah, IA: Dragonfly Books.
Summary: Simple text and playful illustrations explain the differences between wet and dry measurements, weight, length, and size in a fun and relatable context.

Weakland, M. A. 2013. *How tall? Wacky ways to compare height.* Minneapolis: Picture Window Books.
Summary: From the Wacky Comparisons series, this book compares the height of different objects in weird and wacky ways. Also in this series are *How Heavy? Wacky Ways to Compare Weight* and *How Long? Wacky Ways to Compare Length.*

Name: _____

A Letter to the King

Write a letter to the King to convince him to let the apprentice out of jail. In your letter, be sure to

- explain why the bed was made too small for the Queen, and
- tell what the King could do to have a bed made the right size for the Queen.

Your Royal Highness,

_____

_____

_____

_____

_____

_____

_____

_____

_____

Your Loyal Subject,

_____

Name: _____

Measuring the Playground

Can you find something that is…

About 1 centimeter long _____

About 10 centimeters long _____

About 1 meter long _____

Choose some things to measure on the playground. List the object, length, and tool that you used in the table below.

Object	Length	Tool

A Better Way to Measure
to Map a Buried Treasure!

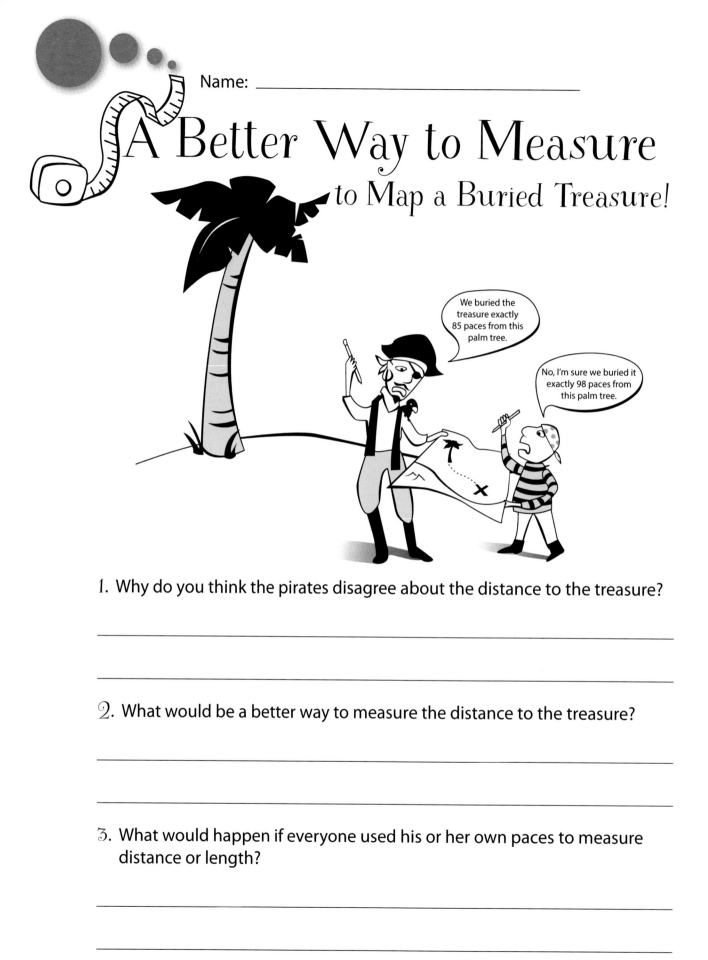

1. Why do you think the pirates disagree about the distance to the treasure?

_____

_____

2. What would be a better way to measure the distance to the treasure?

_____

_____

3. What would happen if everyone used his or her own paces to measure distance or length?

_____

_____

Name: _____

STEM Everywhere

Dear Families,

At school, we have been learning about **the history of measurement**. We measured things in nonstandard units (like spans and paces) and standard units (like meters and feet). We identified tools that can be used to take exact measurements (like rulers and metersticks). To find out more, ask your learner questions such as:

- What did you learn?
- What was your favorite part of the lesson?
- What are you still wondering?

At home, you can watch a music video from PBS Kids about different tools we use to measure.

 Ozomatli: "Measure It!"
www.pbslearningmedia.org/resource/4c3ca5c0-0e33-4504-8a16-f6c29c9730f7/ozomatli-measure-it-pbs-kids-rocks-video

After watching the video, look around at home for tools you use to measure things like size, weight, temperature, and time. Draw and label the measuring tools below. Hint: the kitchen is a good place to start!